HAUNTED HISTORY OF THE UNITED STATES

THE HAUNTED HISTORY OF SAN ANTONIO AND THE ALAMO

BY SUE BRADFORD EDWARDS

Cover image: The word *Alamo* means cottonwood in Spanish. Cottonwood trees grow around the Alamo.

Core Library
An Imprint of Abdo Publishing
abdobooks.com

abdobooks.com

Published by Abdo Publishing, a division of ABDO, PO Box 398166, Minneapolis, Minnesota 55439. Copyright © 2024 by Abdo Consulting Group, Inc. International copyrights reserved in all countries. No part of this book may be reproduced in any form without written permission from the publisher. Core Library™ is a trademark and logo of Abdo Publishing.

Printed in the United States of America, North Mankato, Minnesota.
102023
012024

Cover Photo: Sean Pavone/Shutterstock Images
Interior Photos: Dean Fikar/Shutterstock Images, 4–5, 43; Bill Perry/Shutterstock Images, 6; Shutterstock Images, 9, 12–13, 18–19, 38; Ersler Dmitry/Shutterstock Images, 15; iStockphoto, 20, 23, 25; Kellee Kovalsky/Shutterstock Images, 26–27, 45; Red Line Editorial, 29, 39; M. Timothy O'Keefe/Alamy, 31; Leonard Ortiz/Digital First Media/Orange County Register/MediaNews Group/Getty Images, 34–35

Editors: Priscilla An and Marie Pearson
Series Designer: Ryan Gale

Library of Congress Control Number: 2023939668

Publisher's Cataloging-in-Publication Data
Names: Edwards, Sue Bradford, author.
Title: The haunted history of San Antonio and the Alamo / by Sue Bradford Edwards
Description: Minneapolis, Minnesota: Abdo Publishing, 2024 | Series: Haunted history of the United States | Includes online resources and index.
Identifiers: ISBN 9781098292546 (lib. bdg.) | ISBN 9798384910480 (ebook)
Subjects: LCSH: Haunted places--United States--Juvenile literature. | History--Juvenile literature. | Ghosts--United States--Juvenile literature. | Alamo (San Antonio, Tex.)--Juvenile literature. | Texas--History--Juvenile literature.
Classification: DDC 133.109--dc23

CONTENTS

CHAPTER ONE
The Alamo 4

CHAPTER TWO
The Emily Morgan Hotel 12

CHAPTER THREE
A Haunted Jail 18

CHAPTER FOUR
The Spanish Governor's Palace 26

CHAPTER FIVE
Hauntings Explained 34

Fast Facts 42

Stop and Think 44

Glossary 46

Online Resources 47

Learn More 47

Index 48

About the Author 48

CHAPTER ONE

THE ALAMO

In the summer of 1990, James L. Choron visited San Antonio, Texas, with his children. They toured the Alamo, a historic mission church and outbuildings that had been used as a fortress. They visited the museum and grounds, learning that in 1836 the Alamo was the location of a critical battle in the Texas Revolution (1835–1836). Choron's six-year-old daughter, Megan, was normally talkative and energetic, but on this day she quietly observed her

A battle for Texas's independence from Mexico took place at the Alamo.

There is a memorial near the front of the Alamo dedicated to the fighters who defended the Alamo in 1836.

surroundings for hours. As they left the Alamo, Megan turned and waved. "Goodbye, Jaime," she said.

Choron didn't see anyone, so he asked Megan whom she was talking to. Megan pointed toward the doors. Choron still didn't see anyone and said her new friend must have gone inside.

Megan said Jaime was still there. She described Jaime as 15 or 16 years old. She said he was wearing white cotton pants and a shirt, sandals, and a black hat. Megan said Jaime had accompanied her throughout their visit, telling her details of the battle. Megan said he had been here at the Alamo, the site of the historic battle, for a very long time. Jaime told her he was sad that he couldn't go home but was happy he could talk to Megan. Choron had heard the Alamo was haunted. He believed his daughter had seen the ghost of a Mexican soldier.

OTHER HAUNTINGS

Jaime isn't the only Alamo ghost. Among the most-spotted ghosts is a man wearing a duster coat. Rain or shine, the long coat is dripping wet, and his face is hidden by a cowboy hat. Many people think he was a rider sent out to find help for the Alamo defenders.

A small blond boy can be seen around the gift shop in early February. At other times, a woman appears near the well beside the church. A tall man dressed as a Mexican officer paces the grounds, and a pair of boys sometimes follows tour groups. In March, people sometimes hear a galloping horse in the early morning hours. People believe these ghosts were at the Battle of the Alamo (1836).

THE HISTORY

Long before San Antonio was a city, American Indians including the Comanche (Numunuu) and Lipan Apache lived in the area. Spanish explorers arrived in 1718 and built the Mission San Antonio de Valero. At this time, Mexico and Texas were ruled by Spain. Like other missions, Mission San Antonio de Valero was created to teach American Indian people about Christianity. On May 5,

SOUTHTOWN

San Antonio's Southtown neighborhood was once grungy and crime-ridden. Although it has been cleaned up, the ghosts remain. People say spirits gather at Frank, a restaurant in a former church. Southtown ghosts include Miss Margaret, an actress who announces her presence with the stench of cigarettes and other smells. She is rumored to disappear in a wisp of smoke. Another is Eddie, a boy who tosses things around in the restaurant's basement.

Mission Concepción is another Spanish colonial building that was built in the 1700s.

1718, a presidio, or small military settlement, was established nearby. In 1731, settlers from Spain's Canary Islands arrived and built San Antonio. Lipan Apache and Comanche peoples both attacked the town, and the mission closed in 1793. The buildings became a Spanish military outpost called the Alamo.

In 1821, when Mexico won its independence from Spain, Texas was part of Mexico. The area around

PERSPECTIVES
FIGHTING FOR WHICH SIDE?

Choron assumed the ghost Megan saw was a Mexican soldier. The war between the Texans and Santa Anna is often oversimplified by omitting Spanish-speaking Alamo defenders called Tejanos. "They are the people who often get erased from the story of Texas independence," says James E. Crisp, who teaches in the North Carolina State University history department. Crisp reminds people the fighters on both sides were diverse. "There were free blacks, slaves, Indians from central Mexico who spoke no Spanish, Tejanos, Europeans, including an Italian general," said Crisp.

San Antonio had a small population. Wanting to develop the region, the Mexican government encouraged people from the United States to settle there. Antonio Lopez de Santa Anna was Mexico's president from 1833 to 1836. When he forced these new settlers to pay the same taxes paid by other Mexican states, the result was conflict and warfare. In 1836, Santa Anna led an army into Texas, targeting the Alamo and the fighters inside. Among these fighters were US immigrants and Tejanos. Tejanos were Spanish-speaking Mexicans who had lived in the area before US immigrants arrived. Roughly 200 men defended the Alamo from Santa Anna's army of at least 1,800 men. The fighters held off the army for 13 days before the Alamo fell, and the remaining defenders were executed.

San Antonio is filled with stories of hauntings. Throughout the city, people have reported seeing ghosts of soldiers, civilians, and prisoners. Eerie reports in hotels, jails, and more have been tied to the history of San Antonio.

EXPLORE ONLINE

Chapter One talks about ghosts that people have seen at the Alamo. The article at the website below also talks about Alamo ghosts. What ghosts from this article would you have included in the chapter? Why?

THE GHOSTS OF THE ALAMO
abdocorelibrary.com/haunted-san-antonio-alamo

CHAPTER TWO

THE EMILY MORGAN HOTEL

Another haunted location in San Antonio is the Emily Morgan Hotel. It stands just north of the Alamo, and the historic battle site can be seen from the hotel's upper floors. Hauntings at the Emily Morgan Hotel are based on the building's past.

Built in 1924, the structure was originally the Medical Arts Building, a hospital and office space for doctors. Some people say that psychiatric patients were treated on the seventh floor. Additional tales say that surgeries took place on the ninth floor.

The Emily Morgan Hotel, *left*, **is in the National Register of Historic Places because of its historic significance.**

CREEPY ARCHITECTURE

When the Medical Arts Building was constructed, gargoyles decorated the exterior. Gargoyles are statues of animals or humans that are somehow twisted or distorted. The gargoyles designed for the Medical Arts Building are still part of the Emily Morgan Hotel. Each is a person suffering from a medical problem such as a stomachache or a headache. One even portrays someone who has been poked in the eye.

Many hospitals in the past had morgues in the basement, and people think that may have been the case in this building too. These floors have been the most haunted since the building was converted into the Emily Morgan Hotel in 1984.

HAUNTINGS

Guests staying in the hotel have had a variety of strange experiences. One mother and daughter were getting ready for bed. The daughter was in the bathroom while her mother was in bed. The mother felt a weight settle beside her. She reminded her daughter to turn off the bathroom light. When her

Emily Morgan Hotel guests say they have felt the presence of ghosts in their bedrooms.

daughter stepped out of the bathroom to respond to her, she looked over and saw the shape of someone under the covers beside her. The sheets dropped as the weight lifted off the bed. Uncomfortable with the thought of sleeping where something so strange had happened, the pair requested a new room.

Other guests have odd experiences when they open their doors to step into the hallway. Instead of seeing the hallway, they see the inside of a hospital. When they step back into their rooms, close their doors, and then reopen them, the hospital scene is gone.

Hauntings at the Emily Morgan go beyond sights and sounds. There are also cold spots where the

PERSPECTIVES
NOT KIDDING

Deborah McNabb, sales manager at the Emily Morgan Hotel, checked into a room and then went to dinner. When she returned, she found a bath had been run. "The water was blue. It was so blue that you would actually have to dye this water to be this color. So that was kind of silly," said McNabb in 2021.

McNabb thought another employee was playing a joke. To find out, she had the electronic key card system reviewed. "And they checked it, and my key was the only one that had entered that room," said McNabb. That convinced her that something paranormal had taken place.

temperature is colder in one spot than in the surrounding area. On the fourteenth floor, people sometimes smell bandages and antiseptic.

It isn't just the guests who have had strange experiences. In staff-only areas in the basement, people have heard voices when no one else is there. They have also seen orbs, or round, floating lights. These orbs have also shown up in images taken by the hotel's security cameras. Housekeepers make up beds, leave, and return only to find pillows on the floor.

There are stories of elevators traveling from one floor to another, arriving empty of guests. Sometimes guests enter an elevator and push the button for the floor they want to reach. When the elevator stops and the doors open, the guests aren't at their own floors or the main floor lobby. They are down in the basement, which once held the morgue.

FURTHER EVIDENCE

Chapter Two gives a lot of information about the Emily Morgan Hotel. What is one of the main points that the author makes? What evidence is given to support this point? Now visit the web page below that talks about experiences people have had at the hotel. Find a quote from the website that supports the chapter's point about the hotel. Now look for a quote that provides additional information.

THE HAUNTED HISTORY OF THE EMILY MORGAN HOTEL

abdocorelibrary.com/haunted-san-antonio-alamo

CHAPTER
THREE

A HAUNTED JAIL

Another haunted location in San Antonio is the Holiday Inn Express hotel. This building was once the Old Bexar County Jail. It is located west of the Alamo and the Emily Morgan Hotel. It was built in 1878 because, as San Antonio grew, a larger jail was needed. At this time, a two-story building was built, but the city continued to grow. In 1912, the jail expanded, adding a third floor.

When this third floor was added, the gallows that were used to hang prisoners were

As crime increased in San Antonio, the Old Bexar County Jail was built to house more criminals.

When public hangings existed, many people came to watch.

moved indoors. Before that time, executions took place outdoors. People gathered to watch, and businesses and schools would sometimes close to allow people to attend. By the mid-1900s, executions had been moved indoors. Politicians worried that public hangings had turned into celebrations. Indoor executions were controlled, solemn, private events.

Perhaps the most notorious execution to take place inside the Old Bexar County Jail was the hanging of Clemente Apolinar in 1923. Apolinar was accused of murdering 14-year-old Theodore Bernhard. A medical doctor testified that Apolinar was driven by mental illness to kill. Despite this, he was tried, found guilty, and hanged on February 23.

The jail was expanded again in 1926, creating a total of five floors. An arched entrance was also added. This is still a feature in the building. In 1962, the jail was once again too crowded. Instead of adding onto it again, it was closed and reopened in a new location. In 2002, the original building was converted into a Holiday Inn Express hotel. The hotel was remodeled to include a pool, a fitness center, and a hot breakfast bar, but that didn't erase the building's eerie history.

HAUNTINGS

Like the Emily Morgan, this haunted hotel occasionally has ghosts in its beds. A pair of guests at the converted

Old Bexar County Jail returned from sightseeing and wondered why the bed was rumpled and unmade even though the room had been cleaned. When the dent in the bed disappeared, as if someone had gotten up, the woman put her hand on the bed and felt a warm spot as if someone had been lying down.

But not all the ghosts in the Holiday Inn Express are quiet. One night a guest wearing only his underwear ran into the hotel lobby. He was carrying his bags but hadn't taken the time to dress. While working on his laptop, the

DOING TIME

When the Old Bexar County Jail was first converted into a hotel, the San Antonio Conservation Society contacted the building's owner. Because of the building's historic past, the interior of the building could be changed and modernized, but the exterior had to be maintained. Because of these restrictions, the arched entryway around the front doors remains the same, and there are still bars on the guest room windows.

Ghosts that are able to rumple bedsheets or make noise are called poltergeists.

computer was lifted away from his hands and thrown into the wall. He checked out that night.

Guest rooms, which are where the prisoners' cells had been, are often the focus of the hauntings. Hangings took place between the second and third floors. Prisoners stood atop the third-floor trapdoor. When it dropped open, they fell to the end of the rope.

PERSPECTIVES

NOCTURNAL FOOTSTEPS

YouTuber Jason, of *Diggin with Jason*, stayed at the Holiday Inn Express with his family in 2019. In each room, guests find a page of history about the hotel. After learning more about the hotel's history, Jason and his son decided to check things out at 3:00 a.m. Their room was on the third floor, the floor where hangings took place. "We just got out of the stairwell, there was nobody there, and there were . . . footsteps behind us!" said Jason. "My heart is racing!" said his son. "Right! That's crazy," said Jason as he showed his shaking hand in the video.

People hear whispers and singing at night in their rooms. When they turn on the lights, the voices go silent. Even in the heat of summer, the rooms are often chilly, 15 to 20 degrees Fahrenheit (8.3°C to 11°C) colder than other areas in the hotel.

The staff of the Holiday Inn Express also observe strange events. A manager has noted that motion-activated security cameras turn on when no one is in sight. Once, the

Some people think flickering lights are a sign that a place is haunted.

manager was sleeping at the hotel and was awakened when someone grabbed his arm. He saw no one, but in the morning he noticed a bruise with marks like fingers. It looked as if someone had grabbed his arm.

Lights in the housekeeping area of the hotel flicker and turn off. In addition, at night, housekeepers sometimes see someone approaching the lobby desk. As they walk toward the desk to help this guest, the person disappears. Staff must also reorganize the breakfast area when they find that the room's furniture has been shoved aside or flipped over.

CHAPTER
FOUR

THE SPANISH GOVERNOR'S PALACE

Another haunted San Antonio site is the Spanish Governor's Palace. Near the Old Bexar County Jail, it was built in 1749 as office and living quarters for the various military captains who headed the presidio that protected the local missions, including the Alamo. This building is the only part of the presidio that is still standing. In 1804, the building was sold by the last captain, José Menchaca, to Ignacio Pérez, a merchant whose family went on to live there for 50 years.

The Spanish Governor's Palace is considered a National Historic Landmark.

PERSPECTIVES

HAUNTED OR NOT?

Not everyone on staff at the Spanish Governor's Palace believes in ghosts. Denver Michaels, an author who writes about the paranormal, visited the site. When he asked about hangings that took place there, the employee he was talking to dismissed the idea of hauntings. She stated that no executions had taken place on the site. She said no trees around the modern patio were old enough to have been used for historic hangings. Yet other staff members guide groups through the museum, explaining where visitors have sensed a little girl jumping on the bed or felt a ghostly touch.

Starting in the 1860s, the building was leased and served a variety of purposes. Different businesses rented individual rooms and included a clothing store, a produce shop, and a tailor. One of the renters was even a school.

In 1915, the stone building was in bad shape. Some people wanted to tear it down. Adina Emelia De Zavala was a preservationist. She knew the building was one of the oldest structures in the city and named it the Spanish Governor's Palace.

TIMELINE
OF SAN ANTONIO HAUNTINGS

When people see or hear a ghost, they think about the past. How do you think these events in San Antonio's history contributed to the belief that locations in the city are haunted?

1718 — The Alamo mission and presidio are founded.

1731 — Settlers arrive and found San Antonio.

1749 — The Spanish Governor's Palace, the presidio captain's residence, finishes construction.

1836 — The Battle of the Alamo takes place.

1878 — The Old Bexar County Jail is constructed.

1912 — The Old Bexar County Jail expands to include indoor hangings.

1923 — Clemente Apolinar is hanged at the Old Bexar County Jail.

1924 — The Medical Arts Building (now the Emily Morgan Hotel) is constructed.

The city of San Antonio purchased the building in 1928. Architect Harvey P. Smith studied old photographs and archaeological research. He directed the building's reconstruction. The city restored the original building and added rooms. It opened as a museum in 1931. People still visit to learn about early San Antonio and perhaps encounter a ghost.

HAUNTINGS

Hauntings have been reported in and around the Spanish Governor's Palace since the early 1900s. Near the outside walls, people have spotted the figures of American Indian people. They also saw figures wearing Spanish colonial clothing. Even today, people sometimes walk into cold spots that make the hair on their arms stand on end.

One of the areas where many people claim to see ghosts is the patio near the rear of the building. A local ghost tour company claims that when the presidio was built, criminals were tried and punished there. The worst

Some people feel cold when entering one of the bedrooms in the palace. They think it is the presence of a young girl.

of these criminals were hung from a tree that still grows near the patio. Some visitors say they have seen figures hanging from the tree. Others report orbs in the patio area, often around the tree.

In 2017, a paranormal investigator named Russell Rush brought his crew to investigate the Spanish Governor's Palace. They focused their search on the

THE ELECTRONICS

Russell Rush and his crew used a piece of electronic equipment known as the PX Ovilus to try to listen for ghosts. The crew explained that the device does not pick up actual speech. Instead, it detects energy given off when a ghost speaks. The Ovilus has a dictionary, and it looks up the word that matches that energy level.

courtyard and the bedroom where people sense the presence of two young girls. In the bedroom, one investigator discovered a cold spot. The team recorded a video of what they said was a ghost turning flashlights on and off at the request of Rush's crew.

Rush and his crew reported that the ghost also turned on a light even though the team had unscrewed the light bulb. Their video shows ghosts speaking through equipment designed to pick up disembodied voices. By the well, the device detected the word *soldier*. In the bedroom, it sounded as if the word *help* came through the equipment.

STRAIGHT TO THE
SOURCE

Ghost City Tours runs ghost tours in San Antonio. The company's website talks about the Spanish Governor's Palace. A *comandancia* is a Spanish word for the commander's headquarters.

> *The comandancia was an all-in-one go, where a criminal went to be judged, tried and punished. And it is at the alleged Tree of Sorrows where at least thirty-five of these criminals were hanged for their crimes. . . .*
>
> *During the course of [paranormal investigators'] overnight stay at the Spanish Governor's Palace, they caught multiple orbs around the Tree of Sorrows. So many orbs, actually, that one investigator commented that tree looked completely lit up by all the spectral energy.*
>
> Source: "The Haunted Spanish Governor's Palace." *Ghost City Tours*, n.d., ghostcitytours.com. Accessed 29 Mar. 2023.

CHANGING MINDS

This passage discusses ghosts at the Spanish Governor's Palace. An employee of the museum has contradicted the claims that there were executions held on the site. Take a position on these hauntings. Then imagine that your best friend has the opposite opinion. Write a short essay trying to change your friend's mind.

CHAPTER
FIVE

HAUNTINGS EXPLAINED

People explain hauntings in many ways. Some use history to explain why a spirit might haunt the living. Others try to prove that ghost hunters fake their findings. Still others discuss what it takes to believe in ghosts.

In 2021, the magazine *Psychology Today* reported that 18 percent of Americans claim to have seen a ghost. The magazine interviewed sociologist Christopher Bader, chair of the sociology department at Chapman University in Orange, California. He studies belief in the

Ghost hunters, such as the Southern California Paranormal Detectives pictured here, try to investigate haunted places. They record videos and sounds to detect the presence of ghosts.

paranormal. He told *Psychology Today* that for a place to seem haunted, people must believe in ghosts. If someone believes in ghosts and feels the hair on his or her arms stand up, that person might believe it is a cold spot from a ghost. Someone who does not believe in ghosts would look for a different answer.

David Smailes is a psychologist at Northumbria University in England. He studies why people see and hear things that aren't there. He says people are used to their senses doing a good job. Smailes explains

PEOPLE WANT TO FIND GHOSTS

In San Antonio, people who want to encounter a ghost stop their cars near the railroad tracks at Villamain and Shane Roads. When their cars roll away from the tracks, these people say ghosts pushed them to safety. The story is that a train struck a school bus, and the dead children haunt the intersection. However, in 2003 library archivist Matt De Waelsche found evidence of a train hitting a school bus in 1938. But the accident was in Salt Lake City, Utah. De Waelsche believes this is the accident that inspired the San Antonio legend.

that each person's senses take in only a little bit of the sensory input available. Their brains note the most important information. Then their ears take in the most important sounds, but not all sounds. Their eyes take in the most important colors and shapes, but not all colors and shapes. Then their brains build a scene out of the information. Where there is information missing, their brains fill it in. This is called top-down processing.

When top-down processing works, a person looks at the corner of the room. They see a pile of laundry.

PERSPECTIVES
HOAX OR HAUNTING

Paranormal investigator Vincent Amico reminds people to be skeptical. "Most of that stuff on TV is bunk. It never happens like that," Amico said. Show producers provide content that keeps fans coming back even if it means falsifying something. "A guy says he felt something touch him, or you hear a door slam off camera. That's the easiest stuff to fake," Amico said. He reminds people that ghosts do not show up on demand.

Orbs are often associated with ghosts. White orbs are supposed to be positive, while black orbs are negative.

When top-down processing doesn't work, a person might think the pile of laundry is someone standing in the corner. They know no one could have gotten past them. So they might think they have seen a ghost.

SCIENTIFIC EXPLANATIONS

People claim to have seen orbs at the Emily Morgan Hotel and at the Spanish Governor's Palace. Orbs in photographs and on security camera footage often have a simple cause. Airborne particles reflect light, especially when a camera flash goes off. Photographers call these glowing orbs *glare spots*.

MAP OF SAN ANTONIO HAUNTINGS

This map shows locations in San Antonio that are believed to be haunted. Why do you think these reported hauntings are so close together?

People have felt cold spots at the Emily Morgan Hotel, the Old Bexar County Jail, and the Spanish Governor's Palace. Cold spots can also be explained. People say ghosts absorb heat energy and cause cold spots. Scientists who study thermodynamics know heat cannot be destroyed. Energy removed from one area would create a hot spot somewhere else.

Goosebumps, raised arm hair, and shivers are probably caused by people scaring themselves.

Colin Dickey writes about hauntings and explains the technology used to find ghosts. Prominent among these electronic gadgets is the electromagnetic field (EMF) reader. Ghost hunters believe EMF readers can detect when spirits are present. However, these readers can also detect other things, such as batteries. When a ghost hunter uses a phone to record spectral activity, the phone can also set off the reader.

San Antonio is a city with a long history. Even today, people talk about this history. Many of the stories they tell are spooky. Some people who live in San Antonio have experienced things they cannot explain. Visitors have also encountered things that are spooky or strange. The possibility of finding a ghost is exciting. People will continue searching for paranormal experiences in the city.

STRAIGHT TO THE
SOURCE

Colin Dickey is an author who researches the paranormal. In an article he wrote for the *Atlantic*, he discusses the unreliability of one common ghost-hunting tool:

> The K-II Safe Range is a relatively unreliable electromagnetic field meter. It operates on only one axis (you have to wave it around to get a proper reading), and it's unshielded, meaning that it can be set off by a cellphone, a two-way radio, or virtually any kind of electronic device that occasionally gives off electromagnetic waves. . . .
>
> Erratic, prone to false positives, . . . its flashy LED display will light up any darkened room of a haunted hotel or castle.
>
> Source: Colin Dickey. "The Broken Technology of Ghost Hunting." *Atlantic*, 14 Nov. 2016, theatlantic.com. Accessed 29 Mar. 2023.

BACK IT UP

The author of this passage is using evidence to support a point. Write a paragraph describing the point the author is making. Then write down two or three pieces of evidence the author uses to make the point.

FAST FACTS

- People have lived in San Antonio for 300 years. Battles were fought there, and it is a place where many people have lived and died. People have reported unexplained sights and sounds that they believe are a result of this history.

- The Alamo is one site people believe to be haunted. People sometimes claim to see figures, including children, dressed in historic clothes. In March, people sometimes hear a horse galloping down the street.

- The Emily Morgan Hotel was built as a medical building. People who stay there have reported ghosts in their beds, spectral nurses wheeling carts, and unexplained smells.

- The Old Bexar County Jail is now a hotel. Like the Emily Morgan, ghosts visit the guests' rooms. In addition to lying on the beds, they open windows and sing and speak to people in the dark.

- The Spanish Governor's Palace is now a museum. It was originally where the commander of the presidio lived and had his offices. It is one of the oldest buildings in San Antonio.

- People have reported seeing orbs around the patio in the Spanish Governor's Palace. Some have sensed the spirit of a young girl in one bedroom.

- Ghost hunters claim to have found ghosts throughout San Antonio. They use special equipment that they say can detect voices.

- There are also people who say that many hauntings can be explained. They say that sometimes ghost hunters fake their results. But people continue to look for paranormal events.

STOP AND
THINK

Surprise Me

Chapter Four of this book talks about ghostly happenings at the Spanish Governor's Palace. After reading this book, what two or three facts about hauntings at this location did you find most surprising? Write a few sentences about each fact. Why did you find each fact surprising?

Dig Deeper

After reading this book, what questions do you still have about ghosts and hauntings in San Antonio? With an adult's help, find a few reliable sources that can help you answer your questions. Write a paragraph about what you learned.

You Are There

This book discusses ghostly encounters in San Antonio. Imagine that you are looking for ghosts. What places would you visit? What evidence of ghosts will you see? Be specific as you describe your experiences.

Another View

This book talks about the ghosts people have seen at the Old Bexar County Jail. As you know, every source is different. Ask a librarian or another adult to help you find a second source about hauntings at this jail. Write a short essay comparing and contrasting the new source's point of view with that of this book's author. What is the point of view of each author? How are they similar and why? How are they different and why?

GLOSSARY

archaeological
relating to the study of past human activity, often involving digging up buried evidence

electromagnetic field
an invisible area of energy produced by electricity

gallows
a structure for executing criminals by hanging

morgue
a place, often in a hospital, where bodies are kept

orb
a spherical or ball-shaped object

preservationist
someone who works to save historic buildings

presidio
a protected military settlement

psychiatric
relating to mental illness or the treatment of mental illness

spectral
like a ghost or from a ghost

thermodynamics
the study of heat energy

ONLINE RESOURCES

To learn more about hauntings, San Antonio, and the Alamo, visit our free resource websites below.

Visit **abdocorelibrary.com** or scan this QR code for free Common Core resources for teachers and students, including vetted activities, multimedia, and booklinks, for deeper subject comprehension.

Visit **abdobooklinks.com** or scan this QR code for free additional online weblinks for further learning. These links are routinely monitored and updated to provide the most current information available.

LEARN MORE

Mihaly, Christy. *The Haunted History of Washington, DC*. Abdo, 2024.

Whistler, Jay. *The Ghostly Tales of San Antonio*. Arcadia, 2021.

Williams, Dinah. *Battlefield Ghosts: True Hauntings*. Scholastic, 2021.

INDEX

Alamo, 5, 7–11, 27, 29, 39
Apolinar, Clemente, 21, 29

cold spots, 15–16, 30, 32, 36, 39
Comanche peoples, 8–9

electromagnetic field reader (EMF), 40
Emily Morgan Hotel, 13–15, 16, 38–39

hangings, 19–21, 23, 24, 28, 29, 31, 33
Holiday Inn Express, 19, 21–22, 24

Lipan Apache peoples, 8–9

Mexico, 5, 8–10

Old Bexar County Jail, 19, 21, 22, 27, 29, 39
orbs, 16, 31, 33, 38

presidio, 9, 27, 29, 30

Santa Anna, Antonio Lopez de, 10–11
Spain, 8–9
Spanish Governor's Palace, 27–28, 29, 30–31, 33, 38–39

Tejanos, 10, 11
Texas, 5, 8–10, 39
Texas Revolution, 5
top-down processing, 37–38

About the Author

Sue Bradford Edwards is a nonfiction author who writes about culture, history, and science. She is the author of 30 other titles from Abdo publishing including *Russia* and *Australia*. She lives and works in the Saint Louis area, home of the haunted Lemp Mansion. She has never seen a ghost but does have a cabin near Piedmont, the UFO capital of Missouri.